RETAIL B*TCH

Notes, Rants, ETC... for

Sales Floor Philosophers

Accidental Managers and

Stockroom Lifers

ELIZABETH BEDLAM

Published by Swann + Bedlam

Copyright © 2025 Elizabeth Bedlam

All rights reserved.

part of this publication may be reproduced, distributed, or transmitted in any form or by any means, including photocopying, recording, or other lectronic or mechanical methods, without the prior written permission of the publisher, except as permitted by U.S. copyright law. For permission requests, contact elizabethbedlam@gmail.com

he story, all names, characters, and incidents portrayed in this production ave been changed and have nothing in common (living or deceased), places, buildings, and products

Exterior Cover by
Elizabeth Bedlam

FOR PRIVACY Formatting by Swann + Bedlam
Editing by Swann + Bedlam
an imprint of Punk AF Publishing

WITH PERSONS

Melbourne, VIC 3000
Australia

1st edition 2025 2025 2025

It's Just Retail

Everyone else gets to write about what they do all day, so why not me? I mean, what else am I supposed to write about? I don't climb mountains (scared of heights) or save whales (scared of large things swimming in the sea) on the weekend. I'm not a mommy blogger or a food critic. And writing about writing is the literary equivalent of licking your own reflection. Do I want to be a window licker? No.

I could write about the times I was unemployed or still a student and wanted to walk into traffic out of sheer existential dread, but honestly, who wants to read about my tragic past when I could drag you into my tragic present instead?

Because working in retail, brace yourself, is actually one of the best decisions I've ever made. No, seriously. It's flexible, portable, and everywhere has shops, from mega malls to forgotten strip plazas where dreams go to die. Retail is a job you can take with you when you move cities or countries, or just want to disappear for a bit, and you're starting over. You learn something with every store, every season, every soul-crushing Black Friday sale. You build up a sort of twisted pride from surviving it. A few years here, a few more there, a stint during the holiday apocalypse, suddenly, you're seasoned. Scarred, but seasoned. So why write about retail? Why the hell not? Honestly, the better question is: why are you reading about retail? What are you doing here? Chances are, you're just like me, but don't want to admit it.

Working retail means you failed at life, right? It says that somewhere along the way, something went wrong. You were a teen mom and couldn't get into college. You dropped out and moved home. You are divorced and broke and desperate. Does retail really mean those things? Sometimes but not always. Some of the most insightful, intelligent people I've mean were just working a low-key job in retail, trying to survive the day.

Honestly, most days, a retail job is chill, until it's not. One minute you're standing behind the counter, rearranging chocolate by colour or contemplating whether you could survive if you just crawled under the till and never got back up. The next minute, a co-worker calls in sick, and suddenly you're doing a double shift for the third day in a row. So long, social life! Or you're dealing with a customer who's misplaced his receipt and is now on the warpath because Rex—our crusty, slow point-of-sale system—can't locate his imaginary purchase. He starts hurling legal threats like he's been personally wronged by the gods of retail. Then comes the kicker: he demands to speak to the manager. And with a smile stretched so tight it might snap, you inform him, sadly, you are the manager. The way the light leaves his eyes? Chef's kiss.

Then it's Friday, and instead of a wind-down, you get dragged into some teenage drama between your casual staff member and a girl from another store because someone liked someone else's ex's post on Instagram and now everyone's crying in the stockroom. And just when you think it's over, your phone rings. Head Office is on the line. "Hi! Just wondering what happened in your store today?" You begin praying for a power outage. Or a flood. Or spontaneous combustion.

Yeah, it's "just retail"—that dismissive phrase people throw around like it's nothing. But those of us doing it know better. It can be quiet one minute and full-blown chaos the next. How do you cope? If you love it or just need the paycheck, you push through. That's the gig.

Whether you fell into this line of work by accident and never left, or you're just passing through on your way to something else, or you chose it because, weirdly, you thrive on it, anyone who's ever worked in retail knows it's never just retail. That phrase is the lie we tell ourselves when we want to collapse in the stockroom and cry into the returns bin. It's what I repeat on loop when I catch someone giving me that glazed-over look like I'm a walking cautionary tale just because I'm forty and still asking people if they need a bag.

But I stay. I stay because of the other days, the good ones. The days when I skip home because I nailed a massive sale or turned Karen into a kitten. The customer was happy, I felt useful, and for five seconds, I didn't hate the world. Retail can suck the life out of you, sure. But sometimes, it fills you up again in strange, small ways. Sometimes it even reminds you you're good at something.

Retail is a job. A career. A perfectly legitimate one. It

can be thankless, physically exhausting, and emotionally absurd, but it still counts. It demands multi-tasking, diplomacy, hustle, and a sense of humour. And from outside the display window, where everything looks perfect, no one has a clue what really goes into turning chaos into an unforgetable shopping experience. Unless they've worked it. Unless they've been here.

Just so we're clear: I'm not an expert. I'm not an academic, or an economist, or a motivational grifter with a podcast about "manifesting success in your workspace." I'm not here to promise you the secret to retail Nirvana. I hate those books. I'm just basic. I'm your slightly tired, overly caffeinated store manager in the middle of a busy city. I show up five days a week (or six, depending on who's "sick"), work eight-hour shifts (or longer, if someone tagged the windows again), and hold this whole show together with chewing gum and spite. I'm not selling you a better lifestyle, I'm just telling you about the one you probably already have. Welcome. We're already in the same sad little cult. I'm so excited you're here. We're best friends already!

This isn't a self-help book. There are no morning routines or inspirational quotes etched on minimalist pages. This is a book about retail because it's what I live and breathe and occasionally scream into a pillow about. Writing it is harder than writing fiction, because fiction lets you lie. This doesn't. This is me trying to make something interesting out of customer service and basic pay, and high-up management who forget your name after three years of devoted service.

Why write about retail at all? Most people working it don't love it, and most people shopping think we're NPCs in their consumer experience. To them, we're boring, unskilled, temporary. Or we're losers who couldn't hack it in law school or become brain surgeons. Which is funny, considering I can sell a high-end vibrator while de-escalating a crying junkie and dodging a mystery wet patch in Aisle 3.

This book has been split into a few sections: one for sales associates, the foot soldiers, full of things you can do (and absolutely shouldn't do) if you want to survive your shifts without becoming a cautionary tale. One for managers, to help support their team and maybe keep their own heads screwed on. And one section that's basically just me bitching about stuff. You can skip that, or enjoy it with wine.

What I find in most retail books is that they're written for business owners or people who dream of opening a boutique. Those books are full of crap about advertising budgets, bookkeeping, and HR policies, which are useless if you're working in a chain store with 47000 rules about how to fold a t-shirt. I'll be skipping all of that. You're welcome.

This is for the workers. The part-timers, the full-timers, the lifers. The ones under fluorescent lights who have to ask a manager for permission to go pee. The ones who know the pain of Black Friday firsthand. The ones who've memorised a hundred different ways to say "Sorry, that's final sale." The ones who've had to smile while a customer called them "darling" or "sweetheart" or just barked "Do you work here?" like we don't wear giant name tags.

The store I manage is one of many, stretched across a couple of states. We answer to Head Office, which is just a polite way of saying "corporate overlords." I can decorate the windows and mess with product placement a little, but most things, sales, signage, and branding, come down from above. Working within someone else's vision while still trying to make your space your own? That's a special kind of dance. A tango with spreadsheets and egos and unique visions.

Maybe you'll take something from this. Maybe you'll hate it and dump it into one of those tiny roadside libraries next to a battered copy of *Eat, Pray, Love*. Maybe you'll ditch it for the latest spicy Romantasy TikTok keeps screaming at you about. And hey, no judgment. I can't compete with brooding vampires and teenage witches who become friends to enemies all within 350 pages. All I've got is real life. But I can tell you what to do when the EFTPOS machine dies, three customers are yelling, and someone's just puked near the clearance rack.

SALES ASSISTANTS

Sales Assistants – The Struggle is Retail

We don't all get to strut around in Gucci loafers serving lattes in a glittering luxury boutique. Some of us are behind the counter at an office supply store, hustling pens and paper clips like our lives depend on it. Others might be manning the adult store, navigating awkward conversations about toys no one admits to Googling. And sure, some prefer to be called "client advisors" because it sounds way fancier than "sales assistant," like it might magically elevate your soul or your paycheck. Spoiler alert: it doesn't.

At the end of the day, we're all doing the same thing—selling stuff. And not just selling, but doing it while putting on a show: creating a positive experience, making the customer feel like they're about to make the best purchase of their life, and yes, getting paid before the bills come due. Whether your workplace smells like fresh printer ink, latex, or overpriced cashmere, the skills you need to survive and actually enjoy yourself are the same. You've got to read people, handle weirdos, juggle boredom and chaos, and smile through the nonsense without losing your mind. Master that, and you'll be way ahead of the pack.

Please, Put Away Your Phone

Maybe I'm sounding like the cranky grandma yelling at kids to stop trampling her daises, but good help has always been hard to find. These days, it feels like finding someone who's not glued to their phone is like spotting a unicorn, rare and slightly mythical. If you want to stand out in the sea of tech slaves, here's a simple pro tip: put down the phone. Yes, your manager will notice. Yes, customers will notice. And no, it's not because everyone else is doing it that it's somehow okay.

Phones are the kryptonite of retail. They make you look unapproachable, like you're on a break instead of actually working. Customers see a screen, and they either:

a) avoid you like you've got COVID, or

b) hover awkwardly, unsure if you're going to look up or ignore them.

Neither option wins you any sales or friends.

But it's not just about appearances. Being glued to your phone means you're blind to your surroundings. Who's in the store? What are they up to? Are they browsing politely or planning to steal?

Here's a real-life cautionary tale. This didn't happen at my store, thank goodness, but it could happen anywhere. But at another location, a sales associate, let's call her Anna Banana, was working solo and happily scrolling through her phone when a man walked in. She didn't look up once. Was she too engrossed in TikTok or Snapchat? Or just zoned out? Who knows.

The man wandered around, picked up items, and made sure she knew he was there, but still no reaction. Then came the moment: he picked up an item worth a few hundred bucks, popped off the anti-theft sticker like a pro, and casually walked out the door. Anna Banana? Still swiping and scrolling, not a single word or glance in his direction.

Turns out, the man was a bigwig from head office, running a little "shoplifting test." He called the store owner afterwards to tell him about his successful "theft," then wandered a few blocks to my store, where a staff member, let's call them Jude, was working.

Jude saw him come in, made eye contact, and greeted him like a pro. The exec tried to play the "difficult customer," asking if he could return the item he'd just "stolen." Jude stayed calm, explained our returns policy, and asked if he had a receipt. A few minutes later, the man dropped the act and revealed his head office credentials.

Jude handled it perfectly, professionally, on point, and calmly. I was proud as hell when I found out. As for Anna Banana and the other store? Well, let's just say I had enough on my plate and was than happy for once it wasn't me. Luckily, for the worker, the manager is so damn likeable that she conquered the situation and Anna Banana kept her job. The lesson is crystal clear.

Phones don't just distract you, they drag down the

whole store's vibe. They say, "We don't care, so you can help yourself or leave." I could go on about the culture of phone obsession, from the trainee who took personal calls mid-training to the guy who scrolled Instagram while customers waited. But the truth is this:

If you want to succeed as a sales associate, look engaged and ready to help. You're at work; the internet can wait until you punch out.

Now, what about the store phone? If the floor is empty and the phone rings, by all means, answer it. But if a person is standing right in front of you, wanting to spend their money or even just ask a question, they get your full attention. The person on the phone? They can call back. Your live customer deserves to feel like the most important person in the universe. Because, in that moment, they are.

Bad Day? Leave It at the Door.

Look, we all have days where we want to crawl under a weighted blanket and disappear into a bag of chips and bad TV. Even sales associates. Especially sales associates. But here's the deal: you're at work. You showed up. You're getting paid. So act like it.

Yeah, yeah, it sounds harsh. But it's not. It's maturity. Grown-up stuff. You clocked in, so leave the emotional laundry at home. I'm not saying you have to be some sunshine-barfing rainbow robot, or that you should let customers walk all over you like a human welcome mat. But the brutal truth is: no one shopping for a scented candle or a vibrating cock ring wants to be greeted by the human embodiment of a raincloud. They want someone helpful, upbeat, and ideally not radiating existential despair.

When customers walk in and see you slouched behind the counter, frowning like your dog just died, it sets the tone. They're not going to stop and ask if you're okay. They're not your therapist or your Mom. They'll just assume you hate being there and, by extension, probably hate them too. And honestly? That's fair. Because if you're going to treat the customer like an inconvenience, please stay home. Whatever you're going through is not their fault.

And hey, while we're being honest, maybe the customer is having the worse day. Maybe their best friend died, or their kid just got expelled, or their partner left them for someone with a six-pack and a podcast. People turn to shopping, especially the kind of shopping where the sales associate makes eye contact, for a little relief. A mood shift. A moment of connection. It's not just your job to sell stuff; it's also your job to acknowledge them.

That doesn't mean launching into a TED Talk or trauma-dumping about your own breakup. It just means being kind, being human, and knowing when to engage. A compliment. A small joke. A warm "Hey, let me know if I can help you find something." These are tiny things that don't cost you anything but can mean everything to someone having a rough day.

Want an example? I've got one (lucky you). In my line of work, let's just say we sell very personal items, conversations sometimes get a little raw. One day, a woman came in and just stood there looking lost. She wasn't browsing so much as floating. I approached and asked if I could help. She opened up almost immediately: she'd been married nearly twenty years, and her husband barely touched her anymore. Long-haul trucker. Heavy drinker. Home for two days a week and emotionally MIA the whole time. She felt lonely, unwanted, and confused.

I offered her a few suggestions. Nothing outrageous, just a few things to spark intimacy again. She didn't light up. She just looked at me and sighed. Then she said, "I wish I had your life. You look so happy." That hit me.

So I told her the truth. A few years ago, I was in a dead marriage, too. I cried in the shower. I hated my life. I wanted to vanish. But I made a change. I left. I moved overseas. I started over. I met someone new. Was it easy? Hell no. But it was possible. She smiled, thanked me, and even bought something. Not just because of the product, but because someone treated her like a human being. That moment meant more than the sale.

That's the heart of it: if you work in customer service, you're not just folding clothes or scanning barcodes. You're showing up for people. If you're having a bad day, fine. But your job is to fake it until you feel better. Or at least fake it until your shift ends.

It's not "toxic." It's not "problematic." It's professionalism. It's grace. And weirdly enough, it might actually help you, too. Studies show that helping others, being of service, and being kind can improve your own mental well-being. So no, you're not a robot. But you are being paid to be present, polite, and helpful. That's the gig.

So if you're here, be here. Smile, straighten the shelves, and help someone find their damn shoe size. It might not fix your life, but it just might make someone else's a little bit better.

The Little Things Aren't Little (They're Everything)

This might sound like corporate fluff, but the little things? They matter. Not just in the "aw, how thoughtful" kind of way, but in the this-is-what-keeps-the-whole-damn-store-from-falling-apart kind of way. Good managers see it. Great ones remember it. Even if they don't always say it out loud (because they're probably buried under schedules, reports, and unpaid overtime).

And let's be clear: showing up on time and being available for your shifts are not "little things"—those are the bare minimum. That's what you do if you want to keep your job and not get passive-aggressively removed from the group chat. We're talking about the real little things. Like walking the floor when you arrive instead of spending ten minutes adjusting your name badge and looking bored. Tidy the shelves. Straighten the clothes. Restock what's missing. You shouldn't need a written invitation or divine vision to know the display of soaps and lotions looks like it was hit by a small tornado.

A clean, stocked, organised store helps you as much as it helps customers. Why? Because when someone asks for that purple cardigan in a size Medium, it's a hell of a lot easier to say, "Sorry, we're out," than to panic-sprint to the back room and dig through seventeen half-opened boxes while praying the front doesn't get shoplifted in your absence.

Don't have the item? Cool. Now's your moment to shine. You can say, "We usually get new stock on Thursday, so check back then," or, better yet, take their name and number and offer to call when it arrives. If your store allows holds, set one aside. If there's a chance of a special order, offer to ask your manager and follow up. If the answer ends up being "no," at least you tried. And bonus points if you call them back, just to say, "Hey, we won't be getting that item in again, but I've got a few similar styles I think you might like."

Now you're not just a sales assistant. You're a thoughtful person.

It's about making the effort. Being proactive. Creating a moment of actual human service. Even if you can't perform miracles, you can show people you give a damn, and that's what they remember. Maybe they didn't get the cardigan, but they'll come back for something else because you weren't a useless lump who pointed vaguely and muttered, "Nah, we don't have that."

And don't be afraid to send people to a sister store if you're out of an item they are fixated on. Yes, we all want to keep sales in-house, but if you're out of stock and can't order it, directing a customer to a nearby store isn't a betrayal; it's called customer service. You didn't make the sale this time, but you made an impression.

And while we're on the subject of impressions: you want your manager to like you? Be the person who wipes down the counter, restocks the bags, and takes the trash out without being asked. Be the one who offers to stay an extra hour when someone calls in sick. Even if it's just so your manager can step outside, inhale a cigarette, and cry into a lukewarm 7/11 coffee, it matters. You just bought yourself invisible points that count when scheduling, when promotions come up, and when that beautiful new store opens and needs experienced staff.

Let's talk about handling problems like an actual adult. Say a customer comes in simmering, no receipt, and demanding justice. Maybe their warranty item broke. Maybe their receipt went through the wash. (It happens.) First rule: don't panic. Second rule: don't pass the buck. It's your shift. It's your store right now. Take responsibility.

Start by asking the right questions. "Do you have a bank transaction for the purchase?" Great. Now you've got a date, a time, and an amount. Look it up if possible. Match it with what they say they bought. If everything checks out, reprint the receipt or issue a copy for their warranty claim.

Still need manager approval? Tell the customer you're happy to help and you'll just grab a supervisor. Smile. Thank them for their patience. It's basic stuff, but it keeps things cool. And if your store policy says an item needs to be left for testing or repair, say so clearly, firmly, and without letting yourself get bulldozed. Don't get flustered, don't try to wing it, and definitely don't lose it. Retail's hard enough without creating your own drama.

If the return is possible, process it with grace. If it's not, explain why and offer what you can do. Can you give a store credit? A replacement? A discount on a similar item? Use what's in your toolbox, not what's in your emotional baggage.

And if the customer is yelling? Don't yell back. You're not at a drunken family Thanksgiving with your conspiracy-obsessed Uncle Frank. Stay calm. Stay professional. Your manager will be thrilled, not just because you avoided a meltdown, but because they can actually trust you to run the floor without babysitting.

These aren't small things. They're the things that keep stores running, customers coming back, and you from being just another forgettable name on the roster.

You're Not a Doormat

Here's a shocking truth: customers are not always

awful. Sometimes, they're even... apologetic? They'll sheepishly say, "Sorry for asking so many questions," as if their very presence is a burden and they've just wandered into your private lounge instead of the store you're literally paid to work in. When that happens, it's your job to reassure them, not look annoyed. "No, it's totally fine, that's what I'm here for." Boom. You've just made them feel like they belong, and probably guaranteed a sale in the process.

Most of the time, customers aren't trying to make your life hard; they're just confused, socially awkward, or worried they're being annoying. A little grace goes a long way. Smile. Answer the questions. Show them around. You never know what kind of day they've had before they walked through that door.

But of course, not everyone is a sweet and anxious angel. Some are jerk-offs. Some are confrontational, combative, or just straight-up rude. And when that happens, you've got choices.

Let's get this clear right now: you are not a doormat. But you're also not a fire-breathing dragon. You don't get to torch people because they're being difficult. You stay cool. Stay kind. Stay professional. Never stoop to their level, even if they clearly deserve a few choice insults. Kill them with kindness. Drown them in dignity. They won't know what to do with it.

Let me give you a story. The shop I work in has a setup where the 'staff area' is a square counter, kind of like a mini fortress. Customers come upstairs and usually stop at the first edge they hit. That's not where the register is. So we politely ask them to walk around to the proper side to complete the sale. Simple. Sensible. Nothing weird.

Usually, people do it without fuss. Sometimes they're older or exhausted or confused, and you make exceptions. But we do try, always, to gently direct them to the correct side of the counter. One day, this guy comes in and wants to drop a few hundred bucks on some items. Love that for us. I say, "Sure! Just come around the counter to the register, please."

He looks at me like I just accused him of robbing a bank. "EXCUSE ME?! I've never had to do that before.

WHY?!"

I blinked. He was genuinely offended. Like I'd questioned his integrity or spit in his coffee. So I calmly explained. "There's blind spot on our cameras. For security, especially with large transactions, we ask people to come around to the register. Because if someone runs up behind you, grabs your cash, and bolts, the cameras won't catch much. This is just how we're trained. Its for your safety and ours."

He listened. His expression changed. He relaxed. "Oh... okay. That actually makes a lot of sense."

So he came around the counter and paid. Then—plot twist—as he was leaving, he paused and turned to me. "I'm sorry," he said. "I run training programs for retail teams. I thought you were accusing me of something. But the way you explained that? Perfect. You handled that beautifully."

Personal confession? I hate compliments. I hate apologies. But this guy insisted on giving both. I had no choice but to smile, accept it, and say thank you. I didn't think I'd done anything extraordinary, I just stuck to policy and used a calm, clear tone. But because I didn't get defensive or sarcastic, he left happy. And now? He comes back regularly and spends between $100–$200 each visit. That's called playing the long game.

Now imagine if I'd snapped back. Got mouthy. Took it personally. He would've stormed off, left a one-star Google review, and told everyone I treated him like a criminal. But I didn't. I let him save face, and in return, the business made a loyal customer.

That said, let's be real, if things had gone south, like full-on abusive, threatening, or violent, that's a different story. You don't have to take it. You can and should calmly but firmly tell someone they're being inappropriate and that they need to leave the store. That's your right. That's part of protecting your space and your sanity.

Just know the difference between a misunderstanding and an actual threat. A confused customer doesn't need to be put in their place. A volatile one? Yeah, draw the line. And always document it if it crosses that threshold. Because we're professionals, not emotional piñatas.

And yeah, when it comes to those customers, the jerks, the ones who treat us like we're incompetent trash, we're all secretly thinking, "What a total bitch." We just don't say it out loud.

Learn to Read the Room (AKA The Customer)

Let's be honest: people are losing their ability to read social cues because they've spent the last decade staring into the black hole of their phones instead of having actual human interactions. It's tragic. But if you're working in retail, you need to snap out of it and tune in. Because learning to read your customer is an actual skill, and it'll make or break your day.

Let's break it down. If you greet a customer with a friendly, "Hi! Can I help you?" and they look a little confused and mumble something like, "Umm... I'm just kinda looking," what they're really saying is, "Please help me, I'm overwhelmed and scared I'm going to make a dumb purchase." That's your cue. Don't throw a pitch or corner them in an aisle like a starving retail shark. Say something like, "Yeah, there's a lot to look at! Are you on the hunt for anything in particular?" Keep it breezy. Or toss them a friendly, "If you need anything, just give me a shout! That's why I'm here!" (smile) and let them come to you. Make yourself look helpful, not hungry.

Now, if you get a customer who brushes past you like a cold front and says, "Nah, just looking," or worse, "I know what I'm after," leave them alone. Please. Don't be that associate who circles back every ninety seconds, asking if they've changed their mind about needing help. They haven't. All you're doing is giving them flashbacks to used car lots and timeshare pitch brunches.

There's a difference between attentive and aggressive. You're here to enhance their shopping experience, not pressure them into it like you're on commission for a sketchy kitchen knife company. People remember how you made them feel. And if they felt smothered, condescended to, or manipulated? They won't be back. They'll shop online in their sweatpants with their cat instead.

Which brings us to a slightly touchier topic: human behaviour. Reading people isn't just about sales, it's about knowing when to be friendly, when to back off, and when not to lose your mind over dumb things.

Let's talk pronouns. No one panic. I'm not here to start a culture war, I'm just saying this: if a sweet old man looks at you, sees a person who presents and sounds like a woman, and calls you "miss," don't lose your shit. He's not making a statement about gender politics; he's trying to ask if you carry ankle socks in size 12. And if that ruins your day, you need to toughen up. You're at work, not on a university panel about inclusive language. Let it go. Be cool. Keep your eye on the sale, not the so-called "microaggressions."

And yes, people will say weird, inappropriate things. Some of them will be too chatty, too personal, or socially clueless. That doesn't mean they're dangerous, it just means you need to figure out what's harmless awkwardness versus something actually concerning.

Example: if a middle-aged man is picking out a sundress for his wife and says, "You're about her size, would you wear this?" he's not trying to get in your pants. He's trying to figure out if his wife will look hot in it. He's using you as a fashion barometer, not auditioning you as a mistress. Take it for what it is and move on.

Now, if he starts getting really weird, asking what underwear you wear and if you like lace or leather, okay, that's different. But even then, it might just be awkward guy energy, not predatory. I once had a guy (he was maybe a little drunk) barrage me with lingerie questions, what I liked, what colours I'd wear, how confident I'd feel in something skimpy. I nearly gave myself an eye cramp from all the rolling. But you know what? He wasn't hitting on me. He was dating a new woman, totally clueless about lingerie, and just awkward as hell. When he realised how it sounded, he went beet red. I reassured him it was fine. No crime committed. Just a human interaction gone sideways.

And here's a little side note for the younger girls (but boys, you can listen too): when a guy flirts or calls you "darling," don't act like you've just been handed a trauma. You're not being assaulted. You're being... noticed. It's okay. You can say no without dialling the HR hotline or making a TikTok about it. Why? Because men have been picking up women since forever. It's always been a thing that happens. Always. Before you were born.

If a man asks you out for a coffee, just smile and say, "That's flattering, but I'm at work," or "Thanks, but I have a boyfriend." Even if you don't. It's fine. The world won't end. You're allowed to lie to defuse a weird moment. It's called being street smart. Our mothers did it, our grandmothers did it, and now it's your turn.

When I was 18, I worked in a men's suit store with an old Haitian tailor who made it his life mission to creep on young women. He watched my every move, followed me on smoke breaks to brag about his salary, and invited me to his "private" Christmas party. Ew. Did I file a harassment complaint? No. I handled it. I said I was 18. I said I had a boyfriend. He eventually turned his eye to a girl at Fashion Bug. Was it gross? Totally. Did it ruin my life? Not even close. I left that job, found another, and filed the experience under C for Creeper.

Was it right? No. But life isn't always right. And sometimes a real test is being able to handle weirdness like a grown-up.

Here's the big takeaway: the world is full of people who say weird shit, ask awkward questions, and unintentionally cross lines. That doesn't make them evil. It makes them people. Your job is to read the room, use your gut, and keep things moving. If something truly dangerous happens, deal with it. If someone is just socially tone-deaf, let it go. You're not made of glass.

The more experience you get, the easier this becomes. You'll know who to laugh off, who to ignore, and who to watch like a hawk. Trust yourself. Trust your instincts. And most importantly, trust that you're capable of handling a weird customer without needing a support animal.

You're stronger than you think. And smarter. And if you're reading this, probably a little bit wicked, too—which is ideal for the job. Retail's full of weirdos. Might as well be one of the good ones.

Dress Like You Give a Damn (Even if Your Don't)

Look, we all want to live in a world where appearances don't matter, but let's get real. In retail, they do. That doesn't mean erasing your identity or hiding who you are. You can keep your tattoos, your piercings, your hot pink hair, your dragon-lady nails. All power to you. They are fab! But showing up looking like you've been dragged backwards through a discount bin at the thrift store? Not cute. And definitely not professional.

Here's what this really means: wash yourself and your clothes. If you smell like day-old tacos and last night's vodka shots, nobody's going to buy what you're selling, literally or figuratively. Morning shift? Shower the night before. Not a morning person? Welcome to adulthood, nobody is. Hygiene isn't a personality trait; it's the bare minimum.

And no, your "personal style" does not give you a pass to show up looking like you just crawled out of a wrinkled laundry pile. Crop tops, booty shorts, visible bra straps, gym leggings, UGGs with holes in the toe, save it for your day off, I beg you. You are not here to give your co-workers a glimpse of your underwear or to make customers wonder if you're secretly working your way through a walk-of-shame tour. If you wouldn't wear it to meet your partner's parents or a courtroom judge, don't wear it to work.

Not sure what qualifies as decent retail attire? Start with this: a pair of black trousers and a clean, fitted top. Simple. Timeless. Effortless. Black is your best friend. It hides stains, looks polished, and goes with literally everything. If your pants are dragging on the floor like a sad gothic veil, hem them. Or cuff them. Or tape them up with that hem tape stuff that costs less than your last iced coffee. Just don't let your clothing look like it's given up on life.

Even if your store lets you wear whatever you want, that doesn't mean you should look like you just woke up from a drug binge. You represent a brand, a business, and more importantly, yourself. Comb your hair. Wash your face. Clean your nails. Wear some deodorant. You don't need to go full glam with lashes and contour (unless that's your thing), but a slick cat-eye or some tinted lip balm can go a long way.

Models showing up to go-sees don't come in wearing body glitter and 8-inch heels with their asses hanging out (or maybe these do these days?) They come in clean, simple, and styled so the client can imagine any brand on them. That's you now. You're not selling your own look, you're projecting the image of the store. That image? Approachable, polished, and not actively stinking from poor life choices.

Got a uniform? Great. You can still style it up without looking like a tool. If it's a branded tee, pair it with something cool, black skinny jeans, a cropped blazer, leather trousers if you're feeling fierce. Hell, throw on a leopard print flat and live a little. It's not about being fancy, it's about effort. Clean clothes. Thoughtful touches. That's all.

And can we talk about shoes for a second? You might be tempted try out those sleek new stilettos because they make your legs look amazing. That's cute... for the first 45 minutes. By hour three, you'll be dying inside, and everyone around you will know it. Socks with Crocs? Don't even think about it. There's no shame in wearing stylish flats or low boots that won't make you want to amputate your feet by closing time. Trust me, as someone who made this mistake plenty of times, blisters are not a badge of honour, and they always hurt worse the next day.

Here's the real deal: putting yourself together shows pride. It shows initiative. It says, "I might be making minimum wage, but I still give a damn." And honestly, that energy is magnetic. Customers feel it. Managers respect it. And coworkers, well, they'll either be inspired or silently bitter. That's their problem.

You don't have to be expensive. You don't have to be trendy. You just have to look like you tried. Even if the only thing keeping you sane is a killer outfit and knowing your pants have zero elastic in them, then that's still a win.

Pull it together. You're worth it. And your reflection in the store window will thank you.

Speak With Your Manager

Let's keep this one simple: talk to your manager. I know, sounds obvious, but apparently, it's not. Too many retail workers operate like little ghosts, drifting through shifts hoping someone, somewhere, notices they're confused. Stop it. You are not a haunted Victorian child. Use your words.

You don't have to roll up like you're about to start a union meeting. You can just say, "Hey, can I double-check something with you?" That's non-threatening, friendly, and professional. Most of the time, they'll appreciate it. Even the grumpiest of managers would rather answer a quick question than clean up the mess of a return gone wrong because you misquoted store policy without thinking twice.

Here's what you need to understand: not all managers are good at managing. Some are fantastic. Organised, communicative, supportive. Others... not so much. Some expect you to be psychic. Some leave cryptic Post-it notes like "training thing." (training for what? Hmm...) And some assume because they know something, you must magically know it too through the retail hive mind. Spoiler alert: you don't know. So ask.

And let's talk about the elephant on the phone line: accents. You're not a bad person if you have trouble understanding them. You're not racist, you're not ignorant, you're just a human being whose ears weren't trained to decipher fifteen dialects of English spoken through a $12 phone with a busted speaker. I've been there. I've answered a call, heard a bunch of words through static and poor acoustics, and responded with, "...I'm sorry, could you say that one more time?" twelve times in a row until I wanted to crawl under the register and die. I'm not stupid, the line is bad. I'm sorry.

The worst is when it's someone important, like a head office guy whose voice sounds like it's coming from a tin can at the bottom of the ocean. You're trying to be respectful, but you're sweating and smiling and guessing half of what he's saying. You end the call and you're like, "Did I just agree to a new stock order or give away a kidney?"

Guess what? You're not alone. Just do your best. Ask politely. Apologise, then power through. It's better to look mildly clueless than to pretend you understood and accidentally promise a customer a 30-day refund on a no-return item. Clarify now, or pay later.

Now, what happens when your manager says something that's blatantly wrong? Like, they tell a customer those sweaters are 100% wool and made by a commune of smiling nuns in the hills, but you know (because you're curious, the shift was slow, and you googled it) they're 30% polyester and come from a factory in the frozen hellscape of Siberia. What do you do?

You do not correct them mid-sale. Unless you enjoy public execution, keep your mouth shut in front of the customer. Wait until the moment passes and then, when it's just you two, bring it up casually.

"Hey, I looked up those sweaters online because I thought they were local too, but turns out they're made overseas. Wild, right? Their branding is so sneaky."

Just keep it friendly, like you're both victims of deceptive marketing. This way, they don't feel stupid, and you don't get labelled as that obnoxious know-it-all who thinks they should be running the place. Even if you should.

Sometimes they'll be chill and thank you. Sometimes they'll pretend they knew all along. Either way, you've done your part.

And look, sometimes you will have to correct something more directly, especially if it involves policy that could bite you all in the ass later. When that happens, cushion it. Bring in a third-party scapegoat:

"Oh, remember when the area manager was in? She told us XYZ. I was confused too at first."

See what we did there? You're not saying, "Hey, boss, you messed up." You're saying, "Hey, we were all confused, but this is what we were told." Smooth. Non-threatening. Still correct.

Because at the end of the day, good managers are team players. They don't want to be the emperor with no clothes, strutting around telling lies about wool sweaters while everyone else cringes. They want the store to run well, and you're part of that. When you communicate, you strengthen the team. When you stay quiet out of fear or awkwardness, things fall apart.

You don't have to kiss ass. You don't have to be pushy. But you do have to speak up, ask questions, and correct misinformation gently when needed. That's how adults work together. Welcome to the team.

Working With Sarah

Ah, yes. Sarah. You know Sarah. You've worked with Sarah.

Sarah is that co-worker you don't hate exactly, but you also wouldn't be caught dead getting a drink with her after work unless it was court-mandated. You don't have beef, but her very presence makes you question whether or not you want to opt out of pleasant society all together. She's not evil per say, not malicious, she's just relentlessly annoying. Maybe she overshares about her weird keto diet. Maybe she chews canned tuna with her mouth open in the breakroom like she was raised in a barn. Maybe she's got that perky, overly positive "live, laugh, love" energy that feels like nails on a chalkboard before your second coffee. Whatever the issue, she's there, on your shift, and you can't escape her. That's Sarah.

Working with Sarah is a rite of passage. Every job has one. And unless you're independently wealthy or have a sugar daddy with a yacht, odds are you're going to spend a decent chunk of your adult life trapped in retail purgatory with a Sarah-shaped shadow trailing you through your shift.

Here's the kicker: you don't have to like her. But you do have to deal with her like a grown-ass adult.

Because Sarah isn't doing anything wrong. She's not stealing or being abusive. She's just... Sarah-ing. Which means it's on you to do the internal work of not letting her make your left eye twitch with pent-up irritation. You're not in high school anymore. You can't roll your eyes, gossip in the group chat, and hope she transfers to another store. You've got bills to pay and shifts to survive. That means gritting your teeth and finding a middle ground where you can work side by side without fantasising about staging an "accidental" spill in her general direction.

Now, let's be clear: we're not talking about the truly toxic types. If you've got a co-worker who lies, undermines you, or is trying to sabotage your job, that's a whole other beast, and you go straight to your manager. This isn't that. This is the basic incompatibility of personalities, that classic "I wouldn't sit next to you on the bus, but here we are selling furniture together" vibe.

And this is where small talk comes in.

Yes, I know. Small talk can be soul killing. It's pointless, repetitive, and mostly bland. But small talk is a social lubricant; it's how you get through a 6-hour shift without feeling like you're locked in solitary confinement with a stranger. It's not about making a new best friend; it's about building a tolerable work environment with people.

You don't need to bond over deep existential truths or soul-baring vulnerability. All you need is the ability to fake interest in her Wiccan obsession or the fact she's "re-watching Friends for the sixth time because nothing good is on anymore." You nod, smile, offer a vaguely supportive comment, and then pivot to something neutral like "Did you see that guy earlier who tried to return a candle that was clearly melted in a car?"

It doesn't take much. Retail is full of weird, fleeting moments you can laugh about with literally anyone, even Sarah. Use that. You're both there, you're both clocked in, and odds are you're both low-key dying inside. That's a bond if I've ever seen one.

And who knows? Maybe one day Sarah will surprise you. Maybe she'll cover your shift. Maybe she'll hand you a coffee when you least expect it. Or maybe she'll always be that weird, slightly shrill person who talks too much about astrology, but she still shows up on time and won't leave you hanging when it's time to mop up a spill in aisle three.

In retail, that counts for something.

Sometimes Retail Sucks. But You're Already Dead Inside, So It's Fine.

Here's the thing they never tell you at orientation: retail isn't a job, it's a low-level endurance sport played with barcode scanners and emotional damage. It's not hard in the way people think, it's hard in the soul erosion kind of way. Like water dripping slowly onto the same spot of your brain until all you see when you close your eyes is a flashing SALE sign and

Tom from HR's condescending emails.

Every day is a test of patience and low-stakes humiliation. You'll be accused of ruining someone's birthday because the thing they wanted is out of stock. You'll be told you're rude because you didn't smile enough, and also fake because you smiled too much. You'll have a customer treat you like an actual slug in a name tag, and a manager tell you to "turn the negative into a positive!" like you're some kind of trauma alchemist.

You'll mop up coffee spills, handle some kid's half-chewed rice cracker, and clean a fitting room that looks like someone had an emotional breakdown in it, which they probably did. You'll get blamed for store policies you didn't create, prices you didn't set, and promotions you didn't approve. And you'll say, "I'm so sorry about that," while silently planning your escape route through the emergency exit.

And then you'll do it all again the next day.

But here's the kicker, you'll get really good at it. Not because you love it. Not because you're a people person. But because you're now a hardened retail cockroach, impervious to stress, dead behind the eyes, but still oddly competent. Your customer service voice? Flawless. Your ability to fold a shirt with deadpan resentment? Olympic. You've built an emotional callus where your sense of dignity used to be, and honestly, good for you.

Sure, you'll daydream about quitting. Or faking your own death. Or setting the place on fire and blaming it on a "spark from the faulty card reader." But deep down, you know retail is like a weird, low-budget simulation of real life, and surviving it means you can survive anything. Court appearances. In-laws. Christmas parties.

So no, you don't love it. And no, it doesn't love you. But it's paying (some of) your bills, and that's more than most relationships do. And when the next Sarah annoys you, or the next manager gaslights you, or the next customer tries to return underwear they definitely wore, just remember that you're not here to thrive. You're here to outlast. And that's exactly what you're doing.

So clock out, light a cigarette, and scream into the void if you must. You earned it.

MANAGERS

For Managers

This section is geared toward managers, but hey, anyone can read it. There's no top-secret info here. Maybe you set out to be a manager, or maybe you're like me and just kind of fell into it because, honestly, I don't think one else wanted the job. That's how it felt for me. I hadn't worked in retail for years, and I was convinced I tanked the interview. But somehow, I got hired. During training, I couldn't shake the feeling that I was missing something. Like, there was some unspoken rule everyone knew except me. Spoiler alert: there was. The thing no one tells you? Being a retail manager is hard.

Things I, as a retail manager, am expected to do:

- Show up 5 days a week, maybe more if there is no one to cover a shift.
- Do the rosters, approve leave, ensure all shifts are filled, and that everyone is happy.
- Do weekly sales and performance reports.
- Answer emails from Head Officer Overlords
- Meet with sales reps

- Stock control
- Ordering
- Processing invoices, pricing and putting out stock
- Customer service,
- Cleaning
- Merchandising
- Handle any tradespeople who come in (plumbers, electricians)
- Remove exterior graffiti
- Process return credits
- Keep track of store supplies, orders, and fill said supplies.
- Put up new promos, remove old ones, or ensure someone else does
- Keep everything labelled and organised so that if I get taken, someone else can easily come in and pick up where I left off
- Keep all sales associates informed about any changes, customers, new merchandise, etc....
- If there is a theft issue, deal with it.
- Pricing discrepancies? Hell, leave it for the manag-

er!
- Customer conflict? Refer it to the manager! Because why not? It's not like I'm doing anything else.

There—we might be caught up now. It's not so bad these days, but wow, when I first started? Chaos. I had about two weeks, or roughly four part-time shifts, of training. I'd come home and cry, then rant to my partner. I genuinely wanted to crawl under the sofa and eat my own hair.

After a string of mistakes, a mountain of questions, and one brutally honest meeting with the stock controller and area manager at head office, I finally began to get the hang of things. When my first stocktake came around, I over-prepared like my life depended on it. I fully expected to be chewed out, humiliated, and possibly unemployed by the end of the week. But surprise! It turned out we were actually on the right track. The store was doing okay. I was doing okay.

Staying on top of things is key. And no, I don't mean stomping over your coworkers to climb the corporate ladder. I mean, having a grip on your store, knowing your stock, hiring the right people, and keeping up with the endless parade of returns, negative stock, and paperwork so it doesn't sneak up and bury you alive a week before the end of the financial year.

Do I come home and drink vodka? Not always. But yeah, some days, absolutely. People like to say, "It's just retail." But when it's your responsibility, your store, your paycheck, and your team? It can feel like a lot. Because it is a lot.

Can I Speak To The Manager (Now That's You) - No.

Nothing feels stranger to me than being called "the manager" or "the boss." Every time I hear it, a tiny part of my soul dies. Why? Because it usually means there's a problem, and the sales associate is more than happy to punt that customer my way so I can pretend I've got all the answers. And if someone has to be the one to say "no," guess what? That someone is probably you. Get used to it.

I usually start by listening carefully. If I have to apologise, I do, but I still say no. "I'm really sorry, but no, we can't do that." Whether it's a customer refusing to accept that our return policy is a thing, someone handing you a résumé like it's a golden ticket, or a person asking if you can special-order some obscure trinket from a shop in Albania, the answer is often the same: No. No. No.

Saying no to a customer is an art, and it's all about the delivery. Example: a customer comes in first thing in the morning, trying to return an item they bought the night before. It doesn't fit, or they just don't like it. Can they return it? Technically, no. But instead of shouting, "Absolutely not! Now go away!" I smile, let them explain, and offer a polite, regretful explanation. "I'm sorry—we only accept returns on faulty items covered by warranty. I know, it's annoying. It's a Head Office policy. I really wish I could help." And unless the customer is a total jerk, they'll usually get it. If they start getting aggressive, I direct them to our customer help line, a dusty phone in the warehouse that no one ever answers. But in this case, the customer was chill. We even picked out something he liked better, and it cost more. Shoppers with money and taste? My favourite kind.

Now, let's talk about expectations. Think becoming

The Manager means you're above working the register or asking if someone wants a bag? Yeah, no. You're still very much a sales associate, with a stack of extra paperwork. Fun!

And let's not forget the joy of crushing dreams. When an employee asks for time off they've already been rostered for, sometimes you can make it work. But when you can't? It's another "no." One time, I had a sales associate who'd been working for maybe three weeks ask for the entire week off leading up to Christmas. I thought they were joking. They weren't. "Uh... yeah, that's not going to happen," I stammered, still stunned by the audacity. It's retail. At Christmas. What were they thinking!? They seemed genuinely surprised when I said no. But that's the job. You say no more often than you'd like. Sometimes you feel guilty, but honestly? Most of the time, I don't. Because every time you say yes to something unreasonable, the rest of the team pays the price. Including you.

Give Yourself Some Time

I don't go into work early to look like some kind of

overachiever or to make everyone else look bad. I go in early because when I'm rushed, I make mistakes. I get anxious. And once the day starts off wrong, it just snowballs from there. Most days, everything runs smoothly, but all it takes is one hiccup to throw the whole thing off the rails.

Computer system down? There's 20 minutes gone. Store left in shambles? Add another 30. Taking out the trash or breaking down boxes? That's 10 minutes. Trying to sort out deposit bags, only to find the numbers aren't adding up? Say goodbye to 20-30-40 minutes. The problems add up fast, and the last thing you want is the EFTPOS machine crashing while your banking paperwork is scattered across the counter at opening time. Giving myself that extra 15 (sometimes 30) minutes gives me peace of mind. If something goes wrong, I can deal with it calmly, not in a blind panic.

If you have any say in your schedule and can plan to come in early, you're lucky. At my job, we've got strict start times, and corporate seems to think managers are magicians who can do banking, mop floors, get the tills running, fire up the cinema, and prep the entire store—all in 30 minutes or less. Sure, maybe if everything goes perfectly (except the mopping—that alone takes a good 30 minutes). So instead of stressing, I "volunteer" a bit of my own time for my sanity.

And then there's the shift handover. Whether you schedule staff to come in five minutes early or hang back five minutes after the hour, give yourself that little window to pass the baton properly. It's a good chance to update your team on what's happened, flag any issues, or just check in and see how everyone's doing.

Not Everyone Will Like You

I'll be honest, I'm a pretty private person. I tend to keep my emotions out of the workplace. Only a handful of times in my career have I been so overwhelmed that I needed to step outside for a cigarette and some fresh air. But I know not everyone's like me. Some people need to talk things out, and that's okay. I try to be understanding and listen. Yes, I'm old school, I think you should leave your personal problems at home. But when the problem is a customer or a coworker? That's different. As the manager, it's your job to be available, to listen, and to act when necessary. Even if you don't feel confident, you've got to look confident because if you're calm, your team will be too.

And yet... no matter how hard you try to be fair, steady, and level-headed—sometimes...

You can't be all things to all people, but that doesn't mean you can't be professional. Being an adult means working alongside people you might never choose to hang out with in your personal life.

I don't have much in common with most people. I'm into black metal, extreme French horror films, and I'm a ridiculously picky eater. I don't party, I go to bed by 11 p.m., and I'm up at 5 or 6 a.m. even on weekends. I write books no one reads just because I enjoy it. I love spending time alone. Honestly, I loved COVID. No one expected me to socialize, and it was bliss. I'm not a people person, and yet... I genuinely enjoy working in retail. Why? Because I'm fascinated by people and what makes them tick.

Most of my coworkers over the years have been pretty

different from me. They love hanging out with friends and family, watching wholesome animated movies or boy-wizard franchises. They adore their dogs and pop music, try to avoid being a "hater," and are super politically correct. They're kind, cheerful, likable people. We have nothing in common, and that's okay because it's not like we're getting married. Even if the only thing we share is our place of work, chatting about customers or daily store drama is enough. But no matter how hard you try to get along, you will run into people you just can't vibe with.

One standout for me was back in my early 20s. I worked with a girl a few years older, who I found painfully plastic. She gossiped behind people's backs, then acted sugary sweet to their faces. She called everyone "hun" and "sweetie," was obsessed with Wicca and emo music, and constantly talked about being a lesbian, despite only dating men. She was, in short, a total try-hard. We had our share of clashes, usually when she violated company policy (like lying on the floor mid-shift), showing up late, or just not show up at all.

Still, I kept it professional. I stayed respectful, distant, and tried not to engage, no matter how hard she pushed. She'd gossip about my partner to co-workers, claim he was "too good" for me, and go full passive-aggressive if I didn't open up to her. On "good" days, she'd talk non-stop about her Wiccan rituals for five or six hours straight, and I'd fantasise about throwing myself out the nearest window.

Through all of it, I refused to stoop to her level. I treated her like a co-worker, even when she didn't treat me the same. Thankfully, she quit after about six months. Everyone was relieved, until we hired her replacement. My new challenge? Quietly pulling the new girl aside to have the hygiene talk. Not fun. I'm sure she thought I was an uptight bitch, but seriously, if you're working in retail, you can't come in smelling like body odour, with stained clothes and uncombed hair. That's not judgment. That's just hygiene.

Being a manager means doing the things no one else wants to do. It's not always glamorous. But if you treat people professionally, even when it's uncomfortable, then you've done your part. As someone once told me when I was young, "It's not personal, it's business." I try to remember that.

Never Ask Anyone...

So, how do you stay on good terms with your team when you've got to have uncomfortable conversations and make the tough calls? Simple: don't let your ego get in the way. Sure, you're the manager, but you're still part of the team.

Never ask a co-worker to do something you wouldn't do yourself. It's the holidays, the store looks like a tornado hit it, and you're already running behind at closing time. The bathrooms need cleaning, the fitting rooms are bursting with discarded clothes, the floors need sweeping, and the registers haven't been counted yet. Don't just stand there barking orders, and definitely don't dump it all on the next shift. Delegate tasks fairly, and yes, that might mean grabbing a broom or helping sort out the fitting room disaster. If you've never cleaned the toilet, don't send someone else in there like you're above it. Be hands-on. That's how you earn respect.

Nothing kills morale faster than busting your butt

while the manager stands around chit-chatting. Picture it: you're mopping, folding, hauling in carts, counting drawers and your boss is sipping a coffee, "supervising" from the sidelines. Then they have the nerve to say, "We can't leave until everything's done." In your head, you're thinking, Screw this guy. Time to dust off the résumé.

Here's the thing: acknowledging hard work goes a long way. Team morale matters because if someone's slacking, guess who ends up doing their job? You. Or worse, guess who Head Office tears into because the store looks like a disaster zone? Also you. And they won't be impressed if you try to shift the blame. They'll ask, "You're the manager, why weren't you leading them?"

I always try to show my team a appreciation, especially during the crazy times. It doesn't take much, a bag of chocolates, a candle, something to say thanks. For early morning starts, grabbing 7/11 coffee for everyone who volunteered to come in is a great way to acknowledge your team. Because let's be real: it sucks dragging yourself out of bed at 6 a.m., navigating through ice and snow, only to get mobbed by customers demanding miracles and chewing away at your soul hour after hour. On those days, a box of donuts in the breakroom can feel like a lifeline.

Staying Motivated + Motivating Others

This kind of flows right into the next big topic: motivating your team. Honestly, staying motivated can be really hard, whether you're run ragged because it's been nonstop chaos, or bored out of your mind because it's been dead all day and you're ready to bolt. But staying motivated while keeping your team motivated is crucial.

If I know a shift is going to be slow, I come in with a list of little things I've been meaning to do. If I just stand around, I get bored, my brain starts wandering, and time slows to a crawl. Then when a customer does walk in, I'm low energy, foggy, and can't think of any of the charming, clever things that usually help close a sale.

One of the best pieces of advice I've gotten from managers, owners, and the occasional Corporate Overlord is this: pretend the store is yours. That means tidying displays, fixing up tables, and making the shop look clean, fresh, and easy to navigate.

As you walk around, keep a mental checklist: this display looks half-empty, that one's a jumbled mess, the sale table is an actual disaster. Jump on it. Personally, I love merchandising, it's honestly my favorite thing. The store I'm in now doesn't have a big front window (sadly), but we do have a glass display by the stairs that I get to change every month. Sometimes they don't come out exactly as I imagined, but when they do? And customers start buying directly from your display? That's one of the best feelings in retail.

Merchandising is a great way to stay busy during a slow shift, or when there are just too many staff on the floor. So is cleaning, running a negative stock report, or chatting with customers to build relationships. Don't always try to sell, just talk to them. People are interesting. You'd be surprised how their feedback and opinions can shape how you set up the store or influence your future buying decisions.

Treat the store like it's yours. That means paying attention to the small stuff, replace faded price tags, straighten wall displays, polish up the tables, and check what's selling so you know what needs to be moved or showcased better. These little things make a huge difference.

When it comes to motivating your team, don't micromanage (unless you absolutely have to). Instead, foster a sense of ownership. Things like, "This is our store. Let's make it the one customers want to come back to." I know it sounds petty, but when someone walks in and says, "Wow, this store is way nicer than the other location I've been to," I feel a little surge of pride. Because that compliment belongs to the whole team, we stock what people want, we clean, we're friendly, and we go out of our way to create a great experience.

Staying upbeat, but also realistic, is the best way to connect. Acting like nothing ever gets to you, like you never feel tired or bored, just makes everyone else feel worse. Nothing is more draining than dealing with a line of moody, demanding customers all day, only to have a head office manager breeze in with their triple-shot espresso energy, buzzing around the floor like a motivational speaker on steroids. They chat with customers for five minutes and stick to it. If they keep pushing? Say you'll talk to your area manager and get back to them. It buys you time, and it shuts down the pitch.

You've been trusted with the budget. Spend it wisely. Don't let a pushy rep take control. Don't be afraid to say "No, thank you." And if you're unsure? Just order one or two in the most popular colors and see how they sell.

And one more thing, don't just order what you like. Order what sells. That's the difference between a pretty display and a profitable one.

Stick Up For Your Team

Whether you're defending a sales associate from a cranky customer or from the overlords at Head Office, one thing matters most: have your team's back. You're all in the trenches together, and nothing destroys morale faster than being thrown under the bus by your manager. If a sales associate makes a mistake, it's your job to smooth things over, without calling them out in front of a customer (no matter how boneheaded the error might've been).

Here's a classic scenario: a salesperson tells a customer and then try to lecture you about customer service. It's not inspiring, it's annoying. Be honest. Be human. People will respond better.

Some companies run staff promos, sell 50 units and win a gift card, or get a freebie if you hit a sales target. Personally, I don't find these very motivating because I'm not competitive. I'm motivated by great customer feedback and the challenge of creating the best store environment with what I've got. That said, some people love contests and prizes. It's important to figure out what works for your team. Maybe it's a Starbucks gift card, or buying someone lunch at the food court if they hit a KPI. If you've got a team member who lives for coffee but can't afford it every day, a free Frappuccino might be all it takes to spark some extra effort.

I sometimes struggle to motivate younger staff (mostly those in their early 20s). They just want to be on their phones, texting, watching nonsense, and it drives me nuts. Still, I try to offer genuine praise when they do well. I'll text them after a strong shift or a great sales weekend to say they crushed it. I've also let them take over parts of our social media, which actually works pretty well. If it gets them engaged and motivated, I'm all for it.

Dealing With Pushy Sales Reps

No, not sales reps! Few things are more irritating than a pushy rep trying to upsell you on stuff you didn't ask for and definitely don't want. There's one in particular, from a massage oil and pheromone company, who I dodge every time I see her number pop up on the phone. I know I'll have to answer eventually... but today is not that day.

I hate talking to reps. If you don't watch them like a hawk, they'll sneak all kinds of random crap onto your order. Always—always—go over the order with a fine-tooth comb. I once had a rep email me an order; I politely asked him to remove a few items, and he agreed, then added a snarky comment about how we'd agreed on everything in-store. Um, no sir. I would never agree to order a remote control vibrating kegel egg when the entire existing shelf of kegel eggs is already collecting dust. You can't trust reps as far as you can throw them. They count on you being stressed, busy, or distracted enough to just sign off so they can hit their sales quota and move on. They are salespeople after all.

Don't fall for it. If it helps, have support staff cover the floor while you deal with reps so you can focus. Remember: this is your store. You decide what's worth stocking. Don't let anyone guilt or pressure you into blowing half your monthly budget on stuff that will just sit there. A rep might insist you need a sweater in six different colors, but you know butter yellow and baby blue will never sell in your store, and black and magenta are what's hot right now. They'll probably say something like, "Well, blah-blah store down the road ordered them all today. They're dedicating a whole rack to them!" That's nice for them. But your store is smaller, your customers are younger, and t' want bold, not pastel.

You don't need to be besties with your sales reps need them to show you new stock and help you pla ders, that's it. If the last manager gave them free that's over. You know your store, your custome' actually moves off the shelves. Be direct. Be Have a list of what you actually need befor er they can return a sale item. The customer comes back a few days later wanting to exchange it, only to find out that's not the case. Their voice jumps a few octaves, and boom, manager needed at the counter. Damn it.

Now you've got an annoyed customer in front of you and (if you're lucky) a panicked sales associate lurking behind you. If you're unlucky, that employee isn't even on shift, and now you've got to play retail detective based solely on the customer's version of events. What do you do? You don't say, "Sorry, Jessica gave you the wrong info." Instead, say something like, "It looks like there was a miscommunication, and I'm really sorry about that, but unfortunately, we can't accept sales for return." If needed, blame the computer system. (A harmless white lie. It doesn't have feelings.)

Sometimes the employee is standing right there and owns the mistake. Great. You still don't shame them publicly. Instead, do what you can to make things right, maybe offer 10% off a future purchase, or pass along the customer service number (aka "the number no one answers"). Most people will appreciate the effort. Then circle back with the team member later to go over what happened, clarify the policy, and make sure they understand the issue. Most of the time, it's just an honest mistake from someone who's new or distracted. No big deal, learn and move on. But if the employee seems to not care or shrugs it off? That's when it's time to be firm and explain why it does matter and that repeated issues will have consequences.

The goal is to create a work environment where your staff knows you trust them, so when something goes wrong, your first thought is that it was a misunderstanding, not sabotage.

Case in point: not long ago, I came into work on a Monday to find a lengthy apology from two of my best employees. They'd worked the weekend and were mortified because the store received a scathing online review. Head Office, of course, jumped on it right away.

The review claimed our staff was rude, unwelcoming, and even homophobic toward a queer couple. The accusation? The employees had asked for ID. Mind you, we have signs everywhere stating that ID is required if you look under 25. That's not just a rule—it's policy. Apparently, the couple had been in before and "never had to show ID" (sure, whatever you say). One of them looked quite young, so the staff did their job and asked for ID. They also claimed a group of girls wasn't carded, which wasn't true, they were, just a few moments later when things calmed down.

The two associates in question are not only diligent and respectful, they're also both members of the LGBTQIA+ community. After reviewing the footage and their written accounts, it was clear they'd handled the situation appropriately. The only thing they regretted was not approaching the couple again to ask if they needed help. But honestly? The pair looked annoyed from the start and barely browsed. It made sense that the staff gave them space.

I sent Head Office the associates' statements and didn't grovel. I told them plainly: these two are fantastic with customers, and this was a misunderstanding. Period. Head Office agreed. Our staff is allowed to request ID—it's on the signage, it's store policy, and it's a safety and compliance issue. If anything, the couple were having a bad day and just needed someone to blame.

And let's be honest, if you're over 40, you know being carded is practically a compliment.

Organizing Yourself

As a manager, your brain is juggling flaming swords, between invoices, chasing credits for damaged stock, wrestling with the roster, keeping track of pushy reps, sales reports, and the endless scroll of responsibilities. It's a lot. Overwhelming? Oh, absolutely.

Now, I'll be the first to admit: I'm not as organized as I could be. The store email is a digital war zone. Folders? Never heard of her. But honestly, that's a battle I've chosen not to fight right now. Priorities, darling.

When I first started at this store, it was like a time capsule of madness. It felt like the Gray Gardens of the retail world to put it nicely. Paperwork from five years ago. Hairy dust thick enough to write your will in. Random junk and forgoteen papers shoved under counters, behind shelves, on the floor, truly a clutter connoisseur's paradise. So, bit by bit, during slower moments, I started digging through it. And what did I find? Mostly garbage. Old catalogs, outdated staff forms, expired promos, straight to the bin. In a small store, especially one in an old building, you have to get ruthless with your space. Organisation isn't a luxury; it's survival.

One of the best purchases I've ever made for the store? A label maker. Life-changing. I labelled shelves, cubbies, folders, you name it. The goal? Make life easier for everyone, whether it's a brand-new team member or the poor soul who replaces me someday. Need a hard copy of an invoice from March 2025? Boom—go to the box labelled Invoices, open the March 2025 folder, and there it is. Voilà.

Another game-changer? A giant store diary. I jot down notes at the start of the week—what's new, what to follow up on, what is expiring, what still needs to be done. Staff can write down customer requests, shift updates, callouts, petty theft suspicions, or just passive-aggressive rants about the local buskers. It's a living, breathing log of our retail life, and trust me, a lot can happen in seven days.

When Head Office calls and asks, "When was the last time the aircon was serviced?"—you could squint into the void and guess... or you could flip to March 3rd and find your note: "AC guy was a no-show. No call, no reschedule." Boom. You're not just managing, you're winning.

Being organised also means knowing who did what and when. When staff sign off on orders they've received, priced, and shelved, it's easy to trace issues when (not if) something goes sideways. If twelve items are incorrectly priced, you know who to talk to. Accountability = attention to detail. I sign every invoice I handle and scribble notes all over them—missing items, broken stock, credits issued, emails sent. Date it, sign it, log it.

Now when accounting rings asking why the invoice doesn't match, I don't panic. I grab the invoice, read my notes: "Two broken whatchamacallits—credit issued." I forward the email chain, include the credit note, and shut that case down with the speed and style of a retail detective.

Accidental Manager

So, what's the final word on being a manager? Honestly? It's not for the faint of heart or the easily offended. You're part babysitter, part therapist, part accountant, part janitor, and occasionally an actual manager. You'll be pulled in fifteen different directions before your coffee even cools, and some days you'll wonder why you signed up for this madness in the first place. But when it works? When the team's vibing, the store looks amazing, and customers are walking out happy with their arms full of stuff? It feels damn good.

Leadership isn't about barking orders from behind the counter like some Idi Amin-esque retail dicator. It's about showing up, staying cool under pressure, and making sure the team knows you've got their back—even when things go sideways. You won't always get it right. Some days, you'll snap, spill coffee on the deposit bag, or tell a sales rep to buzz off a little too directly. It happens. Learn from it, laugh at it, and keep moving forward.

Being a manager means wearing a hundred hats and still managing to keep your hair cute. You won't always be thanked, but your impact will be felt in every smooth shift, every well-executed promo, and every team member who starts stepping up because you led by example. So go on, label those folders, sign those invoices, say no to the vibrating kegel eggs, and run your store like the boss you are.

You've got this. Retail may be chaos, but you? You're in control, calm, cool, collected, (most of the time).

ESSAYS

Transgressive Retail

"Why do you work here?" "Why are *you* here?" You'll get asked that in any retail job eventually, but when you work in an adult store, it comes up *a lot*. Apparently, selling sex toys and light bondage gear for a living makes people assume you're also moonlighting as a prostitute or auditioning for amateur porn. While that might be true for a few, most of us are just regular degenerates, students, artists, retail lifers, single moms, part-time philosophers, your standard misfit buffet that ends up in retail for one reason or another, only with better stories and access to discounted Womanizers.

Honestly, if you're going to suffer through a minimum wage job, it might as well come with lube, latex, and the occasional customer asking where the "Beginner Anal" section is. At least you get a laugh, and a solid education in human psychology, fetishes, and what people *really* do when the lights go out. You might suspect that people get up to a lot of weird things behind closed doors, and you'd be right.

And believe it or not, it's fun. People light up when you confidently explain the difference between a dong and a vibrator, how to use a butt plug without ending up in tears, and why mixing silicone lube with silicone toys is the gateway to a gooey disaster. They're *riveted* when you wax poetic about the pleasure and convience of liquid air technology. And let's be honest: people *love* big dicks. They wander over to the Dong Wall, eyes bulging at the 18-inch double-ender, gasping, "Wait... do people actually *buy* these?" Yes. Yes, they do. And I say that with the exhausted serenity of someone who's answered that question approximately 8,000 times in single year.

Once, a group of frat bros asked how I ended up working in a sex shop. I told them the truth: "It's just a retail job." End of story. But in my head? It's the beautiful weirdness of it all. The transgressiveness. The kink. The daily fodder for writing. Why sling overpriced sneakers to uppity teenagers with too much money and too little taste when I could be selling an app-controlled masturbator that moans your name and uses AI to remember your rhythm? That's not just retail that's sexy *poetry* in action.

Of course, not everyone gets it. The judgy types come in, clutching their pearls, asking, "*How* do you work here?" like I'm haunting the counter of a cursed bordello. Like I'm diseased, desperate, and three orgasms from hell. Relax. It's just retail. You're not special for being scandalized.

I remember being told earily on that I was now "part of the sex worker community." I blinked. I sell vibrators to women named Cheryl and lube to accountants named Greg, I didn't realize I had joined a movement. I get the solidarity thing, I do. But most actual sex workers I've met aren't waving some glittery blowjob pride flag. For them, it's work. It pays the bills. They clock in, clock out, and maybe grab a kebab on the way home. It's whatever to me. Its a job, not a lifestyle.

Last Friday a bunch of teens trying to sneak in, shrieking, "Ew, why do you work here?" I was exhausted, dead behind the eyes, and I just snapped: "Because I'm a slut. Now shoo." They spat on the door, and ran off. They grow up so past, the little darlings. They may think it's hilarious, but seriously, they are just one group of dozens of kids to ask the same thing, thinking they are clever as shit when all it does is show their age. Remember when being called "immature" was a insult? When I was 18 if I went into an adult shop I tried to act like *pffff I've seen it all, yeah, I'm an adult*. Now you get 25 year olds squeeling and giggling like they've never touched their girlfriend's boob. What's up with kids today? I am mystfied.

What really grinds my gears, though, is when young people act like anyone over thirty is too ancient to know what sex is, let alone sell toys for it. Hate to break it to them, but older folks are usually having the *most* sex—and the best. Meanwhile, these TikTok toddlers wander in, gawking at the vibrator shelf like it's a crime scene. You're 22 and shocked by a dildo? What were you expecting, scripture and scented candles?

They love to take photos of the toys, yet act like the

whole place is beneath them. Then they slink back a week later to shame-buy a $20 battery-operated vibe. Watching them is like witnessing denial in real time. And they have the nerve to ask *me* what I'm doing here? No, darling. *What are you doing here?*

Then there's the shy clueless-but-curious crowd—early 20s but emotionally 14. They tiptoe in with questions they should've Googled during Year 10 sex ed.

Girl: "My boyfriend's a Dom. I told him I'm a Sub, but I'm not really into it. He's kinda mean about it. What should I do?"

Me *Dump him. You're a person, not a doll.*

Then there's the anal girl complaining about pain.

Me: "What lube are you using?"

Her: "Lube?"

LUBE. How is this still a mystery in 2025? Isn't the internet supposed to teach you things besides dances and how to contour your nose?

Honestly, my *actual* favorite customers are middle-aged couples. You know why they're here. They're confident, curious, and cashed up. They buy the premium toys, the high-end lubes, the genuine leather cuffs—not the sad knockoff kits or cheap vibes that run on two AAs and a prayer. They've got kids, careers, joint tax returns *and* they're still investing in each other's orgasms. *Goals*.

Second favourite? Retirees. The real MVPs. I once had this adorable little grandpa who came in every week, backpack on, ready to drop $200+ on porn DVDs like it was his version of wine tasting. He'd give me a nod, browse the titles, and check out with a smirk and a bag of filth. Bless his heart. Live your truth, sir.

And then... there are the shoplifters. Honestly, who steals sex toys? Or better yet, *who buys* stolen sex toys? They tear open boxes, ditch the charger, and sneak out with a high-end rabbit they can't even power up. What's the plan? eBay? Facebook Marketplace? "Lightly used. No charger. Smells like shame." I've chased some down the stairs. The older men usually cough up the goods, but the younger women? Stone-cold savages. They slither away snakes in the garden.

Working in a sex shop isn't dirty or desperate, it's customer service with a whip and a wink. It's retail with personality. *Transgressive retail*. We help people find their orgasms, their kinks, their confidence. We meet the shy, the curious, the lonely, the pervy, the bored, the regular, and the brazen. And we don't judge. We just sell them things that buzz.

So the next time someone asks, "Why do you work here?" I'll smile sweetly and say, "Because someone's gotta teach your boyfriend how to find your clit. And trust me, with those red cheeks of embarrassment, it's not gonna be you."

Now boys and girls, grab your lube, pay at the counter, and don't forget to buy toy cleaner. You might think you don't need it, but trust me, you do.

Get A job As Soon As Possible

Do parents still tell kids to get jobs? I think I was about 11 or 12 when my mother started telling me to "get a job." As soon as I was legally allowed, 15 years old, she drove me around the local outlet mall while I picked up a dozen applications. There was Claire's, the cheap-o jewelry store every teenage girl shoplifted from at least once. A discount bookstore filled with sad travel guides and untouched cookbooks. The Gap, Old Navy, a Big and Tall store, a lackluster food court, and a rotating door of shops that came and went faster than elderly mall walkers in neon tracksuits.

At the time, I hated it. I hated being forced to smile and act polite. I was a '90s goth who listened to Marilyn Manson and Slayer, and took great joy in scaring the shit out of adults who thought I worshipped Satan and sacrificed babies on weekends. Customer service? No thanks. I tried getting hired at Record Town or Sam Goody, selling CDs, but those jobs were hoarded by the cool college kids. Same deal with the indie bookstores near the MSU campus. Apparently, moody teenagers in fishnets weren't what they were looking for. They wanted 20 year olds with boobs in crop tops and miniskirts.

I hated it then, but looking back, those early jobs, those ones I thought meant absolutely nothing, ended up shaping me. They taught me work ethic and people skills. And I say that as someone who still believes she has *no* people skills. I'm awkward, I hate small talk, and I'd rather eat glass than make a phone call. But when I'm getting paid to show up and interact, I suddenly morph into a functioning human being. Weird, right? I think the shift came from curiosity. I've always been interested in people, why they do what they do, buy what they buy.

In retail, you get a front-row seat to human behavior. Why is this woman dropping $300 on lingerie she'll never wear? Why is that guy buying the stickiest drugstore lube on the market? He must hate his girlfriend. What's going on there? After years of watching and wondering, I've got a stockpile of stories and characters in my head I'll never write down, but will always remember.

But anyway...I drift. First jobs, no matter how

soul-sucking they seem, *matter*. So why the hell don't I see many young people working anymore? Is that contributing to their trash people skills? (Yes, I say this as a person who still avoids eye contact and forgets how to handshake properly. I blame it on being left-handed.) Do teens even *work* now? Are they still being shoved into supermarket bagging gigs and forced to fold shirts at H&M? Do parents still tell their 16-year-olds to go get a damn job?

I mean, if you're going to move out by 18, you need a job, right? Oh—wait. Do kids even move out at 18 anymore? That used to be the dream. Every '90s kid swore, *"When I turn 18, I'm outta here."* Some even fantasized about emancipation at 14. Parents weren't your friends. You didn't want to hang out with them. Even if working at Steak 'n Shake was your only option, the motivation was freedom. You wanted out, and a paycheck was the ticket.

I know, I know, everyone blames AI, smartphones, and "soft parenting" for the death of young people's motivation. But where is the *hunger*? Guys, it's not cool to live at home into your mid-twenties unless you're studying to become a pediatric cardiologist or something. Don't blame unaffordable housing, I've know young people with roommates living in matchbox apartments. If you have to split rent six ways and eat ramen, so be it. Do whatever it takes to unshackle yourself from Mommy and Daddy. Get out of the suburbs!

Personally, it helped that my mother was a crazy bitch. Working at Old Navy or the suit store, measuring sweaty men with too much cologne for funeral suits or fending off pervy tailors, wasn't glamorous. But it got me out of the house. It gave me freedom. It made me proud of myself. And when it's your money, you actually think twice about how you spend it. I side-eye grown-ass adults who blow their cash on vinyl toys and trips to Disneyland. What in the actual hell? That screams "never had a job in high school" to me. No early job, no struggle, no maturity. No wonder young people aren't having sex anymore. They're not adults, they're overgrown toddlers in expensive hoodies.

Working young builds character. It teaches you how to deal with people, pressure, rules, disappointment. I keep seeing news stories about 20-year-olds crying because they are just realizing that they have to go to work every day. Excuse me? Where did these kids grow up? What did their parents do, stroke their egos while spoon-feeding them soft serve? I'm telling you, getting a job as early as possible sets you up. It builds tolerance, skills, industry knowledge. It sets you up for *better* jobs, *less* stress, and a *real* sense of purpose later on.

And if you're shy or have "social anxiety," that's even more reason to dive in. I read something the other day about how some young people are too scared to order coffee in person, so they make it at home on overpriced machines or use apps. WHAT?! Just say you want a damn latte. And if you mispronounce it? So what? That barista's going to talk to 100 people today. You're not a blip on their radar.

I have 20-somethings apologize to me constantly for asking simple questions or taking too long to transfer money to finish their purchase. I tell them it's fine. I forget it instantly. But they'll probably go home and replay it in their heads on a loop, imagining how cringe they were.

So what's an anxious mess supposed to do? I'll tell you,

as someone who *was* (sometimes still is) an anxious mess, but grew up in an era of "get your shit together"—you need to get your shit together. No one is watching you. No one cares. You think everyone noticed that weird thing you said? They didn't. You're not the main character in anyone else's day. That salesperson isn't going to remember your name, your face, or that you stuttered when you asked a question. You only remember customers if they're:

a) Total assholes

b) sweet and nice its shocking

c) really fucking weird

That girl who fumbled with her card at checkout? Couldn't tell you what she looked like. Why? Because it *doesn't matter*.

If you're scared to work retail *because* of anxiety, that's *exactly* why you should do it. Society loves to chant "work on yourself" but pushes therapy as the only answer. Therapy is fine, but in many cases a job is even better. Talk to strangers. Ring up their purchase. Learn to pitch a deal. Learn to take rejection. Learn to laugh it off. The first few shifts might feel like torture, but after a few weeks, you'll find yourself thinking, *okay, I'm anxious, but I can do this*. And that's never something you'll get from therapy or doing 'hot girl walks' where you remind yourself how fucking awesome you are, despite feeling the opposite.

Even now, almost 40, I still remind myself when I feel anxious or out of place: *No one's paying attention*. They're all on their phones. Everyone's wrapped up in their own little dramas. If you trip, if you mess up, no one's clocking it. You're invisible in the best way possible.

Use the crowds as practice. Chat with customers. Throw out a joke. Mess up. Try again. Eventually, the fear fades. 6-12 months in and you'll walk into work like a beast. You'll know the store layout, the policies, the product codes, the vibe. Suddenly, you're not just surviving, you're thriving and you're only 17!

So even if your parents never tell you to get a job, *tell yourself*. Force yourself. If you're scared? Good. That means you *have* to do it. I'm shy. I'm anxious. But when I do the thing I fear? I feel powerful. I feel *in control*.

And I'm thankful for every crappy job I've had. They made me better at the job I have now—a job I actually give a damn about, and, most days, even love.

Killer Boss

By the time I landed a job at a little mom-and-pop gift shop in the mall, I'd already clocked hours in a few different stores. I was 19, broke, and badly in need of a job. This was mid-2005, just before the economy swan-dove off a cliff. The idea of working at the mall, while *not* moving back home, sounded like heaven. After a year of freedom, there was no way I was moving back home.

I was young, a bit lost, and unsure of what I wanted to do. I'd been living off a small inheritance from my late stepdad, but wanderlust had eaten through it. It was time to rejoin the workforce.

I landed the gig at what locals called *the sword store*, located conveniently next to the funeral suit shop where I'd worked at the end of high school. The owners of both stores knew each other and had exchanged notes. I was deemed reliable and quick to learn. I was hired on the spot and told not to wear headscarves, open-toe shoes, or short skirts. Could I wear black? Yes. No problem.

The shop was run by a married couple, let's call them

Jen and Tom. Jen looked like she could be Jennifer Aniston's older sister, and Tom gave off major *Mission: Impossible* Tom Cruise energy. I basically learned how to run a store from them, though mostly from Jen, which was lucky, because Tom was terrifying. I figured he had better things to do than loiter around a gift store changing watch batteries and selling Blade replica swords to nerds. Well, he did. Turns out, Tom had a *very* interesting side gig.

Tom, we eventually learned, worked in some shadowy corner of government, doing something involving the interrogation of terrorists. Air Force? Army? CIA? It's all a little fuzzy, but we *did* see a photo of him strapped to the teeth with about a million weapons and enough ammo to storm a small country. The man had definitely killed people. He was intense and had zero tolerance for errors. A simple mistake could trigger an explosive rant about carelessness, financial losses, and our general ineptitude. As a staff of mostly young women, we quickly developed a shared mission: *never* piss off Tom.

Still, we stifled giggles when he stormed into "the back" to rant to Jen about idiotic customers. "The back" was just a flimsy partition near the rear of the store, doubling as an office, watch-repair nook, and engraving station. You could easily hear him calling someone a dumbass. Customers would glance at the wall, wondering if he meant them, then quietly leave. This was another reason he mostly let Jen handle things. Tom wasn't what you would call a people person.

When Tom and Jen argued, "the back" transformed into their personal war zone. Shouting would erupt, followed by Tom storming out the back door, and Jen muttering curses under her breath before reappearing with a forced smile. "Never go into business with family," she'd say, then immediately follow it up with: "Never open a small business. It sucks. You never get a day off. I haven't taken a vacation in over ten years! Listen to me, girls: *never* start your own business." We all nodded solemnly, even though that *was* exactly what I wanted to do, despite the tanking economy and the rise of internet shopping.

Doing inventory with Tom was an actual nightmare. He'd print off stacks of paper detailing the expansive Zippo lighter numbers in the stockroom. They'd been selling

Zippo for over several decades, and the back room was a Zippo graveyard. Counting them all took days. I'd dream about those little lighters and then return the next afternoon to count them again. No mistakes allowed. If you said there were three pink Playboy Zippos, there had better be exactly three. Not two. Not four. Three. Otherwise, you got the dreaded lecture about your "sloppy work" and how it was ruining everything and putting his business in serious jeopardy. I learned to go slowly, double-check everything, and document it perfectly, because the alternative was worse.

And what about when Jen and Tom went home for the night? That's when *we* were in charge of engraving things—Zippo's, plaques, whatever needed to be personalised. God help you if you made a typo. The dread of messing up someone's name was unmatched. You'd leave a note apologising for the mistake, and by your next shift, if Tom was there, you'd get a soul-piercing glare and a lecture so sharp it could etch glass. "Take your time. Mistakes like this should never happen again. Do you understand?" Cue clenched jaw. Cue internal panic.

Tom was short—maybe 5'5" or 5'6"—but *scary*. He'd seen things. He'd done things. Even Jen didn't know where he went or what he did during his "other job." And yet, when he returned in a suit and aviators, with slicked-back hair and a grin, we all agreed he had the same disturbing look a dog has after a successful squirrel hunt. His blood lust was satisfied... for now.

Eventually, Tom seemed to tire of international interrogation work and decided to take on a new challenge: law school. Because obviously, being terrifying in one career wasn't enough. Despite being older than most students, he thrived and graduated at the top of his class. Last I heard, he was running for local District Attorney. Given his cold, unflinching predator eyes, I'm sure he'll go far.

So, how did working for this duo prepare me for life? At the time, I thought Tom was completely unhinged. But I also realised he taught me procedure, and why it exists. That fear of messing up shaped me. I learned to slow down, be deliberate, and always double-check my work. You didn't want to knock over a trinket because you were rushing. So we cleaned those endless rows of glass cabinets slowly, carefully—mantel clocks, crystal figurines, decorative knives, and, of course, Zippos. So many Zippos. They still haunt my dreams.

Sure, I still mess up sometimes, miscount something, forget a task, but thanks to my bootcamp-like training in that mall gift shop, it happens way less. I learned how to stay organised, follow instructions, and document everything. If something went wrong, we could always trace it back. Accountability was built in.

In a twisted way, having a boss who was capable of murder turned out to be the best on-the-job training I could've asked for. I left that store practically bulletproof. Multiple employers have since described me as "low maintenance." I don't complain. I stay busy. There's always something to clean, organise, or learn. I earn my paycheck. Just don't ask me to count Zippos ever again.

Aggressive Customers
– What Can You Do?

Dealing with aggressive customers can go one of two ways: either you stay calm and in control, or it spirals into chaos and you're left dealing with the aftermath. And let's be real, if you're a young woman and the customer is a loud, older dude built like a brick shithouse, it can be especially intimidating. So, how do you handle it?

Last week, I got a call from a shaken co-worker. She'd just had a run-in with an aggressive customer that has terrorised our stores in the past. She needed someone to cover her shift because she had to get out of there, and I really didn't blame her. Yet at that moment, I had customers browsing and couldn't talk much, so I said I'd message the others. One was in class, the other asleep.

It got me thinking: why do some stores seem like magnets for lunatics? Sure, our sister store across town gets more trouble, bad location, unlucky mojo, cursed land or whatever, but after chatting with a mental health nurse and reflecting on my own lovely little horror show of retail experience, the answer became clearer.

I speak to everyone the same way, whether they look like a meth gremlin or a dentist on his lunch break. Friendly, respectful, even-toned. I grew up with an unpredictable mother who could explode over the way you said "okay," so I learned early how to keep things smooth, non-threatening, and boring.

And I've noticed a trend: the sassier my co-workers are, the more chaos they seem to attract. Some people can't handle pushback, especially if they're high, mentally unstable, or just the antisocial dregs of society. If you come at them with an attitude, they don't back down. They double down. They'll scream, steal, lie, threaten, piss on the floor, throw shit, whatever it takes to "win" the interaction.

Once, a man came in, clearly tweaking with matted hair, cracked lips, eyes like dinner plates. But he greeted me, asked for a product, and when I didn't have it, I pointed him to another store. We had a brief, weirdly civil chat. He wandered around, found his reflection in a mirror, had a full-blown argument with himself, and left. No drama.

Ten minutes later, he was up the road at our sister store, in full rage mode. Why? Probably because their manager, while kind, hilarious, and sharp as hell, doesn't suffer fools. Her sass met his psychosis, and boom: fireworks. He went from a cooked weirdo to a mouthy demonic force in record time. And honestly, it tracks.

It's like dealing with a toddler mid-tantrum; you don't start screaming too. You stay calm. Steady. Boring. That's how you win. Or at least, how you don't lose.

Let's break it down with a case study:

A drunk guy walks in, open bottle of wine in his hand. What do you do? You don't yell, panic, or clutch your pearls.

You: "Oh, sir, I'm sorry—we don't allow drinks in the store." (smile, be chill)

Him: "Huh?"

You: "You can leave it here at the counter if you'd like."

Him: "No..." (starts walking in)

You: (still polite) "Sir, no drinks allowed. You're welcome to come back after you've finished it."

Him: "That's bullshit. I always drink in here."

You: "Maybe, but it's store policy. Our other staff will tell you the same; it's not just me."

Him: "I just wanna look around."

You: "Totally get it. But drinks have spilled on products before we have to follow the rules. Leave it here and I'll help you find what you need."

You treat him like a human being. Stay kind if possible. And—key move—blame the rules. Say it's policy. Say Head Office insists. Invent a terrifying manager named Brenda if you need to. The point is: don't poke the bear.

I'll admit that doesn't always work. We have been threatened with drunk, bottle-wielding street people before. It ended with us saying the police had been called, and he had better leave ASAP. Luckily, that worked... otherwise it could have been much scarier.

One girl told me a woman on meth once tried to shoplift, threatened to set her on fire, then came back weeks later like nothing happened. She had to be shown footage just to convince her she was banned. Amnesia by meth, oh what a lovely gift.

If someone comes in who's previously stolen or caused

chaos:

You: "I'm sorry, but you're not allowed in. You've stolen from us in the past."

Them: "What? That's not true!"

You: "Okay so how about we call the police on Blah Blah Street? You can review the footage with them. If I'm wrong, they'll let me know." (They have never called my bluff on this.)

Them: *[crickets]*

And just like that, they vanish. Nobody wants to chat with the cops.

This works beautifully on mouthy teenagers, too: "I know, it sucks, but we can't let you in. It's a $20,000 fine (probably a lie). Take it up with the police if you want." Boom. Scene over, usually...

The whole point is: don't escalate. If they're shouting, you keep your tone steady. Repeat your message like an automated voicemail from hell. Blame fake policies. Blame Head Office. Hell, blame Nancy in HR. Just don't let their chaos become your chaos.

Repetition is magic, especially with people on substances or in a full-blown episode.

"I'm sorry, you can't bring drinks in."

"It's store policy, we can't allow drinks."

"You can shop, but you'll need to leave your drink here."

Yes, in your head, you're thinking: screw you, hope you fall into a sinkhole. But on the outside? You're an unbothered, laminated employee-of-the-month poster girl. Calm. Unmoving. Dead behind the eyes, yet somehow charming.

Pro tip: When it's teens, hit 'em with your inner Mom. Calling them "boys and girls" or "children" wounds the soul. If a 16-year-old's acting tough, I'll beam and say, "Sorry, children, come back when you're old enough!" and you can see the existential crisis bloom behind their eyes.

That said, once an 8-year-old cussed me out like a trucker on speed. So I grabbed his arm and walked him out. He yelled, "You can't do that!" and I said, "Go tell the police." He didn't. That was the end of that little darling. Oddly enough, he did return with a friend a week or so later, and they were pretty chill about not being allowed in. They asked where I was from, we chatted for a second, then they left to go drive someone else insane.

At the end of the day, you're not just a cashier or stocker, you're a security guard, therapist, negotiator, and low-budget exorcist. Aggressive customers are just part of the retail circus, but you don't have to hand them the whip. Stay cool. Keep your voice flat. Repeat yourself like a glitching NPC. Blame Nancy or Sarah. Blame the computer.

You're trying to survive your shift with your dignity intact and your store un-smashed. Let them yell. Let them sob about their human rights being trampled because you wouldn't let them bring a Slurpee into your high-end French lingerie boutique. Just smile, nod, and escort them to the exit with the cold grace of a retail war veteran.

It's 5 pm on a Friday. You've been here eight hours. You're not paid enough for this. And yet—you handle with grace. Because *you've seen things* and you know you'll see many more before you retire.

Check Out

Have you ever worked in a chain store during that cursed stretch of time between Black Friday and New Year's? If you have, then you already know. The lines. The chaos. The crying children and the grumpy shoppers, clutching their Starbucks in one hand and fistfuls of plastic bags in the other. Everyone wants a deal, but it's never good enough. They complain about prices, about stock levels, about your existence. You stutter an apology you don't mean, because what can you actually do?

I was 15 when I was thrown to the wolves on the floor of Old Navy in South Central Michigan. It was an outlet mall, which meant the shoppers were somehow cheaper and crankier than average. We didn't carry the same selection as the big mall stores, but that didn't stop people from blaming *me* personally for the lack of sequined crop tops or dog sweaters.

We wore scratchy, blue Old Navy tees with khaki pants (also from Old Navy, mandatory, of course). My manager was a college student. Nicole? Nikki? Something with an "N" and a nose ring. She had kinky red hair and gave off a "broke art major who listens to riot grrrl" vibe. I felt extremely lame around her and the rest of the older, college-aged staff. I just did what I was told.

Clean the changing rooms? Check. Fold endless piles of waffle-knit thermals and graphic tees? Sure. Float aimlessly around the store until someone needed assistance? Fine. These were all tolerable. It wasn't until they stuck me on the register that I thought, *Christ, I need to get the fuck out of here.*

Until that point, the worst customer I'd dealt with was a woman demanding to know where the dog clothes were.

"The Old Navy in Lansing has them," she said.

"Well, then... go there?" I thought. Out loud, I smiled and said I'd check the back, even though I knew damn well we didn't carry dog clothes. We were an *outlet*. We carried clearance basics, unsold overflow, and the tears of fast fashion interns. Still, I put on the headset, asked anyway, then walked into the back room, stood around for five minutes like I was on a spiritual quest, and returned.

"Nope, nothing hiding back there either." She huffed

and insisted I was wrong, then sighed dramatically and announced she'd "just have to drive all the way back to Lansing." Yes, please do. Hurry. Go. Right. Now.

But the register? That was hell. They placed me at the very last register at the far end of the row, as far from the head of the line as physically possible. I'd wave my arm and yell, "Next!" over and over while shoppers just stood there, blank-faced, staring straight ahead like checkout zombies. The people in line would start poking the one at the front, nudging them like, "Go! She's calling you!" Eventually, after enough whispering and gesturing, they'd look startled, offended, even, and shuffle down like I'd just spoken in tongues. Sorry, ma'am. Next time, I'll send a carrier pigeon and escort you down personally. It's not like I'm doing anything else.

One especially miserable December day, around 5 p.m.—I'd been working since opening—I was again yelling "Next!" to no avail. No one moved. I stood there, waving like an inflatable car dealership guy, wondering what the hell I was supposed to do. The line was rapidly growing and yet no one was interested in moving.

Then a woman at the *end* of the line looked at me and said, "Can I just go since no one else is?"

I glanced at the lifeless corpse at the front of the line. Still motionless. Still waiting for divine instruction. Deaf to my gestures. For I knew, dead to the world.

"Yeah, sure," I said. I didn't even feel guilty about it. She had two items. She'd be in and out. She rushed over, grateful, and I started scanning her purchases.

That's when a zombie in the middle suddenly reanimated.

"Hey! Why does *she* get to go!?"

I gestured vaguely toward the woman now halfway through checkout and said, "Because no one else was moving?"

"Where's your manager!?"

With a sigh, I pointed to Nikki (Natasha?), who promptly came over. I saw wild hand gestures and finger-pointing as the shopper raged about my treachery, how I had dared to serve a willing customer while they stood there doing *nothing*.

The woman I'd served gave me a whisper of thanks and

fled out the nearest door like a fugitive. They were not going to make her go back in that line.

Did I break the rules? Maybe. But also, maybe people should take a little responsibility for being so passive and dumb. Just... pay attention when you're waiting in line. Do I need a damn flare gun? I was 15, wearing heavy black eyeliner with chopped-up hair, filled with loathing for most of humanity. I silently dared the lady to try to get me fired.

Nikki (Nina? Nunchuck?) came over and asked what happened. I told her the truth-ish: no one was moving, and the woman at the end was the only one who looked even vaguely interested in, you know, *buying* something. I shrugged. "I didn't know..." I lied. She didn't care. She nodded, sighed, and assigned someone to stand at the front of the line to direct traffic to the other 9 registers. *Pathetic*, I thought. Humans are hopeless.

And honestly, I still think that today.

Have you ever been caught in the hive of people trying to use the self-checkouts? It's called *SELF* CHECKOUT, yet they'll stand, frozen, staring at the machines, waiting for a bored-looking staff member to wave them forward like they're air traffic controllers. Why? What the hell is going on?

My local grocery store has this ridiculous bottleneck of candy displays and junk you're forced through just to reach the checkouts. It's narrow, awkward, and people will come to a full stop in the middle of it, either to examine a Snickers bar or because there's no employee to give them permission to move. It drives me insane. The checkout area is wide open. You can see *all* the registers. You could literally just walk to one and start scanning. And yet, they just stand there.

It's gotten so bad that my partner and I have started cutting them off entirely. They stand frozen, waiting for nothing, while we breeze past them and go to one of six empty registers. We don't even feel guilty anymore. If you're going to act like you need a hall monitor to buy your pasta and tampons, that's on you.

Has anyone else experienced this? Is it just me, screaming internally in the aisles like a retail war veteran?

Here's the thing: it's not hard. Walk to the empty checkout. Scan. Pay. Bag. Leave. You don't need someone to hold your hand. This isn't a trust fall exercise. Every time I witness this strange, sheep-like behaviour, I think to myself: *This is it. This is the end of civilisation. We're in our swan song. If you can't even manage self-checkout, maybe we deserve extinction.*

So please, dear shoppers: when you're next in line, *act like it*. If you're going to use the self-checkout, actually *use it*. Get your card ready. Move when it's your turn. The rest of us would like to buy our stuff and go home before the sun explodes.

A Pretty Penis

I've seen more dicks than I care to count. Working at a few adult venues when I was younger stripped me of my horror real quick. I once had to walk in on a girl mid-wank job (oh, I'm sorry, a *sensual massage*) to politely ask if she was almost done, because another guy was waiting his turn.

That job was dirty. It was sleazy. I left it fast. I briefly danced, I suck at it, and I left that too. But now I work at a different adult store, still not exactly PG, but comparatively? A palace. The place is clean, the customers are mostly pleasant, and the air doesn't reek of regret and stale lube. You get all sorts: old men with shaky hands, bright-eyed 18-year-olds buying their first toy, nervous couples, even the occasional grandma who pretends she's buying "a back massager." But then... There are *those* customers. I'm not talking about the junkies or the shoplifters, they're their own flavour of chaos. I mean the *inappropriate* ones. The ones who treat the store like a public extension of their bedroom. Guys rubbing one out with a hand in their pocket. Someone trying to jerk off in the DVD section. Or all those dudes in the porn cinema, quietly stroking away in the dark while I'm apologising that the projector's on the fritz and it'll just be a second and I'll be out of there. Mean while in the dark, they lurk just over my shoulder, dicks out, waiting impatiently.

But then... *he* walked in. The man with the most beautiful penis in the world. Well, according to him.

It was a quiet night, around 11 PM. My coworker was sorting DVDs, I was dusting dildos, and in he strolled, late thirties, suspiciously tanned, with a thick Eurotrash accent and the swagger of a man who'd just discovered mirrors.

Him: "Do you have cock rings?"

Me: "Yes, we do!"

I led him to the display, proudly presenting our diverse ring collection. He barely glanced at it before launching into a detailed monologue about what he was *really* after: something big, something thick, something that hugged both shaft and balls, a figure-eight design. Alas, we were fresh out. But he was far from done.

Him: "This is what it looks like."

Out comes his phone. He starts scrolling.

Him: "Do you go to Sexpo?"

Me: "No, haven't had the chance."

Him: "This photo was taken at Sexpo. By an artist. She photographs genitals to normalise sexuality. This one is mine."

And there it was. On his phone screen, a high-resolution close-up of his cock bound in a ring. To me, it looked like a dick, any dick. Not big or small, just a dick.

Me: (attempting attemping to keep my composure) "Yeah, um, we still don't have that style."

But he wasn't listening. He was lost in the magic of his own member.

Him: "Everyone said my cock was *beautiful*. Even the photographer said it was the most beautiful cock she'd *ever seen*."

Me: "Hm."

He rambled into a reverent retelling of the praise he received at Sexpo. Women swooning. Men patting his back, "Hey bro, nice cock." I mentally checked out. No matter how often I tried to shut it down, he just kept going, singing hymns to his glorious schlong. I silently wondered why these things always seemed to happen to me.

Mid-monologue, a woman came in and shoplifted. My coworker and I tried to stop her, but she was gone in a flash. This momentarily distracted him from his penile passion project. I thought he was going to leave, but then turned to me once more.

Him: "Do you have transparent underwear for men?"

Me: "We have these."

I showed him our selection. Naturally, nothing was good enough. He whipped out his phone again to show me a photo of himself in sheer briefs, his dick smooshed inside like a cocktail sausage trapped in cling wrap.

Me: "Yeah... nothing like that here. Sorry."

I gently nudged him toward the idea of another store, but he was too busy reliving the glory days of people falling in love with his penis. Finally, it was closing time. I walked him to the door. He said he'd be back tomorrow for the porn cinema. *Fabulous*. I thought it was over. He descended the stairs. I wandered behind the counter.

Then I heard footsteps. He was coming back up. Inside, I died a little. What now?

Him: "By the way... would you like to get coffee with me?"

For the record, I declined. Coffee should always come before you meet the dick. No matter how pretty they claim it is.

www.ingramcontent.com/pod-product-compliance
Lightning Source LLC
Chambersburg PA
CBHW011613290426
44110CB00020BA/2584